TRUMPisms

TRUMPisms

COMPILED BY SETH MILLSTEIN

INTRODUCTION BY BILL KATOVSKY

Skyhorse Publishing

Visit our website at www.skyhorsepublishing.com.

10 9 8 7 6 5 4 3 2 1

Library of Congress Cataloging-in-Publication Data is available on file.

Cover design by Rain Saukas

Print ISBN: 978-1-51071-095-5
Ebook ISBN: 978-1-51071-096-2

Printed in the United States of America

"The following pages will be straightforward and succinct, but don't let the brevity of these passages prevent you from savoring the profundity of the advice you are about to receive."

Donald Trump, introduction to *Trump: How to Get Rich*

Table of Contents

Introduction

We must first thank Donald Trump for turning the 2016 Republican presidential nomination into a reality television show. He learned well from hosting *The Apprentice*. His wealthy celebrity status automatically earned him a seat at the table—or rather the important podium during the debates. His poll numbers have defied gravity like unobtainium on the moon Pandora in *Avatar*. Republican rivals are wary about criticizing him. Nor do they want to become his punching bag during a news cycle. He *is* the elephant in the Republican green room. For someone ranked as the 121st richest person in America, according to *Forbes*, his campaign feels manic and go-for-broke, with the conventional political playbook disregarded.

This has given Candidate Trump tremendous freedom to speak his mind. Rather than go into specific details about foreign policy (Middle East in flames) or domestic policy (income inequality), Trump prefers generalities that appear half-baked and nonsensical. His presidential announcement speech at his Trump Tower office building in Manhattan on June 16, 2015 was pure theatre—wacky, digressive, narcissistic, entertaining. Many memorable lines emerged from his announcement: "I will be the greatest jobs president that

God ever created. I tell you that," or the very endearing "I don't need anybody's money. I'm using my own money. I'm not using the lobbyists. I'm not using donors. I don't care. I'm really rich." There was the reminder that "When Mexico sends its people, they're not sending their best. They're not sending you. They're not sending you. They're sending people that have lots of problems, and they're bringing those problems with us. They're bringing drugs. They're bringing crime. They're rapists." And the question everyone was wondering: "When did we beat Japan at anything? They send their cars over by the millions, and what do we do? When was the last time you saw a Chevrolet in Tokyo? It doesn't exist, folks. They beat us all the time."

The announcement speech also served another function: it showed that the media-savvy Trump was truly the first uncensored and shoot-from-the-lip Republican candidate. The more outlandish the sound bite, speech, or tweet, the better chance Trump had in dominating the news cycle. It's why his poll numbers started fairly high, and continued to creep higher, making him the frontrunner. He took his celebrity recognition and leveraged his brand. Instead of affixing his name to hotels, golf courses, and casinos he rebranded himself as the savior of America by adopting an anti-Washington, political outsider, and ultimate-fixer platform.

To solidify his alpha standing in the crowded Republican field, the real estate tycoon decided not to play nice. He insulted and belittled his rivals, mocked members of the media, and became an even bigger braggart.

Long before he had political aspirations, Trump always made for colorful copy in a variety of ways: in his bestselling books ("For many years I've said that if someone screws you, screw them back. . . . When somebody hurts you, just go after them as viciously and as violently as you can," *Trump: How to Get Rich*, 2004); in magazine profiles ("I'm intelligent. Some people would say I'm very, very, very intelligent," *Fortune*, April 3, 2000); and in television interviews ("Part of the beauty of me is that I am very rich," on ABC's *Good Morning America*).

To his making-it-up-on-the-fly credit, Trump elevated his game in the summer of 2015. That is why the book you are holding is called *Trumpisms*. This book collects the best of The Donald's outlandish, over-the-top quotes. Here are his own unscripted words.

But first, why is this book named *Trumpisms* and what exactly does the title suggest? Its provenance owes a debt to former Slate.com's editor Jacob Weisberg's bestselling books, *Bushisms* and *Palinisms*. He wrote in the introduction to the 2008 vice president nominee's book, that *Bushisms* "often hinged on a single grammatical or factual error. *Palinisms*, by contrast, consist of a unitary stream of patriotic, populist blather. It's like Fox News without the punctuation."

Trumpisms stem from the boastful expression of megalomania and scene-stealing hubris. Trumpisms are typically short statements combining bombast and pompousness, factual inaccuracy, and theatrical showmanship, and are at their best when employed as insults.

Trumpisms borrow from that fancy-shmancy French art term "*trompe l'oeil*," which references something that tricks or deceives the eye. The Donald is also a deceiver, a master flimflammer. He has zero interest in holding fast to the facts or truth. He is well-versed in the overlapping regions of twaddle, bosh, and trickery. He will say virtually anything at any time. For Trumpisms to excel, they need to override discretion and tactfulness. Trumpisms avoid the teleprompter or notes. That's because no living soul on this planet is as smart, sexy, intelligent, or wise as Donald Trump. He will also be the first to tell you.

Trumpisms can be divided into five categories: 1) rude, boorish comments; 2) clownish pokes in the ribs; 3) statements of self-regarding conceitedness; 4) impertinent put-downs; and 5) statements of macho arrogance or racism. The method of delivery for Trumpisms is through media interviews, his books and speeches, debates with Republican rivals, and tweeting. There is no other presidential candidate who has so heavily relied on Twitter to bad-mouth and taunt opponents.

It's been almost thirty years since that famous line "where's the beef?" was used in a presidential race. Former Vice President Walter Mondale borrowed that line from a Wendy's ad campaign in the 1984 Democratic presidential nomination to describe the policies of his opponent Senator Gary Hart. With Trump being interviewed, giving a speech, or obsessively tweeting, his remarks appear associated with a different hamburger chain, as they're quite a whopper!

Don't expect Trump to rein in his towering ego. Nor to see him speak in politesse and behave like a thoughtful, serious-minded pol. When you're as outlandish and supersize as Trump is (or thinks he is), there is little to almost no chance of quietly receding from view, even in defeat. He will take his Godzilla act to the Republican National Convention in Cleveland next summer, turning that quadrennial event into yet another political reality television show.

The media put up with the crazy antics of Trump because he drives television ratings, boosts the sale of newspapers and magazines, and increases Web traffic. The media's attitude toward Trump is a hold-your-nose affection—like having your super-rich uncle, who owns a chain of car dealerships, show up for Thanksgiving dinner in a blinged-out white stretch limo with a third wife half his age. A columnist for the *Chicago Tribune* once asked, "I wonder how many times he can put his foot in his mouth before he chokes to death?"

At his most elemental core, Trump is a master entertainer, a larger-than-life role he honed following a skein of lucrative real estate deals in the eighties and nineties and several bestselling books. That kind of early success and publicity fueled a vanity as sizeable as the multi-story Trump Tower in midtown Manhattan.

While it's difficult to calculate his current net worth, *Forbes* placed it at 4.5 billion dollars, far below the $10 billion figure Trump originally paraded before the media. His business track record is hardly sterling: hundreds of millions of dollars were lost as a result of four casino and hotel bankruptcies.

These losses affected his personal net worth and tarnished the Trump brand. His campaign slogan, "Make America Great Again," could just as easily have been "Make Trump Great Again."

No one can accurately predict the future, and that is so true with presidential politics. What we do know is that Trump has totally disrupted the Republican field. Should he eventually win the primary, what next? The general election will be that much more unusual and fun to watch. Should he ever make it to the White House, the first presidential executive action will probably be renaming it the Trump House.

—Bill Katovsky

On Domestic Policy

"I think if this country gets any kinder or gentler, it's literally going to cease to exist."

Playboy, March 1990

On Taxes

"The messenger is important. I could have one man say, 'We're gonna tax you 25 percent.' And I could say [to] another, 'Listen, you motherfuckers, we're gonna tax you 25 percent.' Now you've said the same exact thing. You've said the same exact thing, but it's a different message."

Campaign event, Las Vegas, 10/08/15

On Immigration

"We're rounding 'em up in a very humane way, in a very nice way. And they're going to be happy because they want to be legalized. And, by the way, I know it doesn't sound nice. But not everything is nice."

60 Minutes, 9/27/15

On Syrian Refugees

"What I won't do is take in two hundred thousand Syrians who could be ISIS. . . . I have been watching this migration. And I see the people. I mean, they're men. They're mostly men, and they're strong men. These are physically young, strong men. They look like prime-time soldiers. Now it's probably not true, but where are the women? . . . So, you ask two things. Number one, why aren't they fighting for their country? And, number two, I don't want these people coming over here."

Face The Nation, 10/11/15

———

"This could be the greatest Trojan horse. This could make the Trojan horse look like peanuts if these people turned out to be a lot of ISIS."

Face The Nation, 10/11/15

On Border Control

"You wouldn't be hearing about the word immigration if it weren't for Donald Trump. I brought the whole subject up!"

Interview with Katy Tur, NBC News, 7/08/15

"I will build a great, great wall on our southern border, and I will have Mexico pay for that wall. Mark my words."

Campaign launch rally, 6/15/15

"It will be a real wall. It'll be a wall that works. It'll actually be a wall that will look good, believe it or not. Cause what they have now is a joke. They're—they're ugly, little, and don't work."

60 Minutes, 9/27/15

"I said, we need to build a wall and it has to be built quickly. I don't mind having a big, beautiful door in that wall so that people can come into this country legally."

Fox News Republican debate, 8/06/15

On September 11th

"I think I could have stopped it because I have very tough illegal immigration policies, and people aren't coming into this country unless they're vetted and vetted properly."

Hannity, 10/20/15

On Education

"Twenty-five countries are better than us at education. And some of them are, like, third-world countries."

Campaign launch rally, 6/15/15

———

"[Overseas] we build a school, we build a road, they blow up the school, we build another school, we build another road they blow them up, we build again. In the meantime we can't get a fucking school in Brooklyn."

Speech in Las Vegas, 4/28/11

On Infrastructure

"We're becoming a third-world country because of our infrastructure. . . . You come into LaGuardia Airport, it's like we're in a third-world country."

Campaign launch rally, 6/15/15

On How He'll Help Women

"I will be phenomenal to the women. I mean, I want to help women."

Face the Nation, 8/09/15

———

"I cherish women. I want to help women. I'm going to be able to do things for women that no other candidate would be able to do."

CNN's State Of The Union, 8/09/15

———

"I will take care of women. I respect women. I will take care of women."

CNN Republican debate, 9/16/15

On Women in the Workplace

"I have really given a lot of women great opportunity. Unfortunately, after they are a star, the fun is over for me."

ABC's *Primetime Live*, 3/10/94

———

"I have many women that work for me."

Face the Nation, 8/09/15

———

"She's not giving me 100 percent. She's giving me 84 percent, and 16 percent is going toward taking care of children."

TIME, 5/23/11

On Gay Marriage

"It's like in golf. . . . A lot of people—I don't want this to sound trivial—but a lot of people are switching to these really long putters, very unattractive. . . . It's weird. You see these great players with these really long putters, because they can't sink three-footers anymore. And, I hate it. I am a traditionalist. I have so many fabulous friends who happen to be gay, but I am a traditionalist."

New York Times, 5/01/11

On Race

"I have a great relationship with the blacks. I've always had a great relationship with the blacks."

Albany's Talk Radio 1300, 4/14/11

———

"Sadly, because president Obama has done such a poor job as president, you won't see another black president for generations!"

Twitter, @realDonaldTrump, 11:45 a.m., 11/25/14

———

"Our great African American President hasn't exactly had a positive impact on the thugs who are so happily and openly destroying Baltimore!"

Twitter, @realDonaldTrump, 12:38 a.m., 4/28/15

———

"I have black guys counting my money ... I hate it. The only guys I want counting my money are short guys that wear yarmulkes all day."

Conversation with John R. O'Donnell recounted in
*Trumped: The Inside Story of the Real Donald Trump—
His Cunning Rise and Spectacular Fall*, 1991

———

"I have a great relationship with African Americans, as you possibly have heard. I just have great respect for them. And they like me. I like them."

Anderson Cooper 360, 7/23/15

———

"A well-educated black has a tremendous advantage over a well-educated white in terms of the job market. . . . [I]f I were starting off today, I would love to be a well-educated black, because I believe they do have an actual advantage."

NBC News interview, 1989

On Health Care

"The U.S. cannot allow EBOLA infected people back. People that go to far away places to help out are great-but must suffer the consequences!"

Twitter, @realDonaldTrump, 5:52 a.m., 9/02/14

———

"Healthy young child goes to doctor, gets pumped with massive shot of many vaccines, doesn't feel good and changes - AUTISM. Many such cases!"

Twitter, @realDonaldTrump, 5:05 p.m., 3/28/14

———

"I am being proven right about massive vaccinations—the doctors lied. Save our children & their future."

Twitter, @realDonaldTrump, 9:30 a.m., 9/03/14

———

"If you can't take care of your sick in the country, forget it, it's all over. I mean, it's no good. So I'm very liberal when it comes to health care."

Larry King Live, 10/08/99

On the Environment

"We'll be fine with the environment. We can leave a little bit, but you can't destroy businesses."

Fox News Sunday, 10/18/15

———

"It's Thursday. How much money did Barack Obama waste today on crony green energy projects?"

Twitter, @realDonaldTrump, 3:54 p.m., 10/18/12

On Global Warming

"It's really cold outside, they are calling it a major freeze, weeks ahead of normal. Man, we could use a big fat dose of global warming!"

Twitter, @realDonaldTrump, 9:30 a.m. 10/19/15

———

"Sorry, folks, I'm just not a fan of sharks – and don't worry, they will be around long after we are gone."

> Twitter, @realDonaldTrump, 7:26 a.m., 7/04/13

———

"NBC News just called it the great freeze – coldest weather in years. Is our country still spending money on the GLOBAL WARMING HOAX?"

> Twitter, @realDonaldTrump, 6:48 p.m., 1/25/14

———

"This very expensive GLOBAL WARMING bullshit has got to stop. Our planet is freezing, record low temps, and our GW scientists are stuck in ice."

> Twitter, @realDonaldTrump, 7:39 p.m., 1/01/14

———

"The concept of global warming was created by and for the Chinese in order to make U.S. manufacturing non-competitive."

> Twitter, @realDonaldTrump, 2:15 p.m., 10/6/12

On How He'll Create Jobs

"I'm going to bringing back great numbers of jobs from China, from Japan, from India, from Brazil, from so many countries that have been just absolutely stealing our jobs."

Face the Nation, 11/08/15

On Veterans

"We've got to take care of our vets, our vets are being treated—our vets are being treated so badly. You know, I brought up the subject of illegal immigration, right? Our vets are, in many cases, being treated not as well as illegal immigrants."

South Carolina rally, 10/19/15

On Gun Control

"No matter what you do, guns, no guns, it doesn't matter. You have people that are mentally ill. And they're gonna come through the cracks. And they're going to do things that people will not even believe are possible."

Meet The Press, 10/04/15

On Eminent Domain

"I say eminent domain is something you need. . . . If I build a highway, and if something's in the way of the highway, you're going to have to do something with that."

Fox News Sunday, 10/18/15

On America

"We need very strong people, because our country is being taken away. It's like candy from a baby."

The Herd with Colin Cowherd, 11/02/15

On American Leadership

"We have very stupid people in our country negotiating for us, and we have leaders that don't know what they're doing."
Interview with Katy Tur, NBC News, 7/08/15

————

"People say, 'Oh, you don't like China,' No, I love them. But their leaders are much smarter than our leaders. . . . It's like take the New England Patriots and Tom Brady, and have them play your high school football team. That's the difference between China's leaders and our leaders."
Campaign launch rally, 6/15/15

On President Barack Obama

"If Obama resigns from office NOW, thereby doing a great service to the country—I will give him free lifetime golf at any of my courses!"
Twitter, @realDonaldTrump, 11:52 a.m., 9/11/14

————

"Why is Obama playing basketball today? That's why our country is in trouble!"

> Twitter, @realDonaldTrump, 6:48 a.m., 11/06/12

———

"Obama is the great divider, he has totally used race. And it should have been the other way around."

> *The Economist*, 9/03/15

———

"The way President Obama runs down the stairs of Air Force 1, hopping & bobbing all the way, is so inelegant and unpresidential. Do not fall!"

> Twitter, @realDonaldTrump, 5:23 p.m., 4/22/14

———

"We have a president who doesn't have a clue. I would say he's incompetent, but I don't want to do that because that's not nice."

> Fox News Republican debate, 8/06/15

On President Obama's Reelection

"We can't let this happen. We should march on Washington and stop this travesty."

> Twitter, @realDonaldTrump, 7:59 a.m., 11/07/12

"This election is a total sham and a travesty. We are not a democracy!"

Twitter, @realDonaldTrump, 8:03 a.m., 11/07/12

On President Obama's Birth Certificate

"He doesn't have a birth certificate, or he hasn't shown it.... His grandmother, in Kenya, said he was born in Kenya, and she was there and witnessed the birth.... He has what's called a certificate of live birth. That is something that's easy to get. When you want a birth certificate, it's hard to get."

Interview with Meredith Vieira on Today, 4/07/11

"An 'extremely credible source' has called my office and told me that @BarackObama's birth certificate is a fraud."

Twitter, @realDonaldTrump, 4:23 p.m., 8/06/12

"Obama finally gave his birth certificate. And I got such credit for that, because I accomplished something that nobody else had accomplished."

Speech in Las Vegas, 4/28/11

On Great American Leaders

"Winston Churchill was an unbelievable leader. Why? He was born with a speech impediment, he had all sorts of problems, he certainly wasn't a handsome man, and, yet, he was a great leader. Why was he a great leader? Nobody knows."

Larry King Live, 10/08/99

———

"[Jesse Ventura was] definitely the strongest governor in the history of the world, because he was able to lift 350 pound men over his shoulders and drop them into the fourth row, and very few people can do that."

Larry King Live, 10/08/99

On What Defines America

"This is a country where we speak English, not Spanish."

CNN Republican debate, 9/16/15

On the Greatness of America

"Our country is in serious trouble. We don't have victories anymore. We used to have victories, but [now] we don't have them. When was the last time anybody saw us beating, let's say, China in a trade deal? They kill us. I beat China all the time. All the time."

Campaign launch rally, 6/15/15

———

"No matter what country you're talking about, they beat the United States."

Virginia rally, 10/14/15

On International Affairs

"Our leadership is weak and pathetic. I mean, we can't even beat Libya."

Campaign event in Las Vegas, 10/08/15

On International Dealings

"I deal with the Chinese, I deal with Turkish, we just made a big deal with Turkey. I deal with a lot of the people in the world. They cannot believe—they tell me, they're friends of mine— they say, 'We don't believe what we're getting away with.'"

The Situation Room with Wolf Blitzer, 12/08/11

On Mexico

"I love Mexico. I mean, Mexico, I have thousands of people from Mexico that work for me. Thousands. Hispanics."

The Economist, 9/03/15

———

"They're sending people that have lots of problems, and they're bringing those problems with us. They're bringing drugs. They're bringing crime. They're rapists. And some, I assume, are good people."

Campaign launch rally, 6/15/15

———

"Our leaders are stupid, our politicians are stupid, and the Mexican government is much sharper, much more cunning. [So] they send the bad ones over because they don't want to pay for them, they don't want to take care of them."

Republican presidential debate, 8/06/15

———

"I'm not angry at Mexico. I'm angry at our leadership for not putting our right people to negotiate this."

Interview with Katy Tur, NBC News, 7/08/15

On China

"I know the Chinese. I've made a lot of money with the Chinese. I understand the Chinese mind."

Xinhua, April 2011

———

"First of all, I love China. The people are great. They buy my apartments for $50 million all the time. How could I dislike 'em, right?"

Virginia rally, 10/14/15

On Japan

"Who is our chief negotiator? Essentially it is Caroline Kennedy. I mean, give me a break. She doesn't even know she's alive."

The Economist, 9/03/15

———

"You know the pact we have with Japan is interesting. Because if somebody attacks us, Japan does not have to help. If somebody attacks Japan, we have to help Japan. That's the kind of deals we make."

The Economist, 9/03/15

———

"I have tremendous respect for the Japanese people. I mean, you can respect somebody who's beating the hell out of you."

The Oprah Winfrey Show, 1988

On Russia

"I think that I would probably get along with . . . [Vladimir Putin] very well, and I don't think you'd be having the kind of problems that you're having right now."

Face The Nation, 10/11/15

———

"Who was I on with on *60 Minutes*, do you remember? Putin! He was my stablemate. We got tremendous ratings."

South Carolina rally, 10/19/15

On North Korea

"We have this mad guy [Kim Jong-un], I guess he's mad. Either he's mad or he's a genius, one or the other, but he's actually more unstable, even than his father, they say. They said the father was a pleasure by comparison to him, in North Korea."

The Matt Murphy Show, 8/21/15

On American Allies

"I'm interested in protecting none of them unless they pay."

Campaign event in Las Vegas, 10/08/15

On the Iraq War

"What was the purpose of this whole thing? Hundreds and hundreds of young people killed. And what about the people

coming back with no arms and legs? Not to mention the other side. All those Iraqi kids who've been blown to pieces."

Esquire, August 2004

———

"You know, in the old days—I'm like an old-fashioned warrior. The old days, when you had a war and you won the war, it was yours."

Campaign event in Las Vegas, 10/08/15

On the Middle East

"Saddam Hussein is gonna be like a nice guy compared to the one who's taking over Iraq. Somebody will take over Iraq, whether we're there or not."

The Big Idea with Donny Deutsch, 2006

———

"You have Iran—is going to take over Iraq. I called that many years ago on your show. I said, we shoulda never gone into Iraq, which I should be given a little credit for vision."

O'Reilly Factor, 9/28/14

———

"They [Saudi Arabia] want to go in and raise the price of oil, because we have nobody in Washington who sits back and

said, 'You're not gonna raise that fuckin' price, you understand me?'"

Speech in Las Vegas, 4/28/11

———

"I dealt with [Muammar] Gaddafi, I rented him a piece of land. He paid me more for one night than the land was worth for the whole year, or for two years, and then I didn't let him use the land. That's what we should be doing. I don't want to use the word 'screwed,' but I screwed him."

Fox News, 4/21/11

On Oil

"You take the oil. It's simple. You take the oil. There are certain areas which ISIS has the oil and you take the oil, you keep it. You just go in and take it."

The Economist, 9/03/15

On Fighting Terrorism

"When you see the other side chopping off heads, waterboarding doesn't sound very severe."

This Week with George Stephanopoulos, 8/02/16

"If you look at Saddam Hussein, he killed terrorists. I'm not saying he was an angel, but this guy killed terrorists."

The Big Idea with Donny Deutsch, 2006

"I have an absolute way of defeating ISIS, and it would be decisive and quick and it would be very beautiful."

Interview with the *Des Moines Register*, 6/02/15

"I think ISIS, what they did, was unbelievable what they did with James Foley and with the cutting off of heads of everybody, I mean these people are totally a disaster."

60 Minutes, 9/27/15

"If you look at Syria. Russia wants to get rid of ISIS. We want to get rid of ISIS. Maybe let Russia do it. Let 'em get rid of ISIS. What the hell do we care?"

60 Minutes, 9/27/15

On Osama bin Laden

"Tell me, how is it possible that we can't find a guy who's six foot six and supposedly needs a dialysis machine?"

Esquire, August 2004

———

"I don't know why Obama gets credit for the whole bin Laden thing. He's sitting there. He's got three choices: Leave him alone—which nobody would do—take him out with a missile, or take him out with the military. So he said, take him out with the military. OK. Congratulations."

The Situation Room with Wolf Blitzer, 12/08/11

On His Campaign

"I have no intention of ever running for president."

TIME, 9/14/87

On Whether He'd Run for President

"I doubt I'll ever be involved in politics beyond what I do right now."

> Interview with Larry King at the Republican National Convention, NBC News, 1988

"I don't want to be president. I'm 100 percent sure. I'd change my mind only if I saw this country continue to go down the tubes."

> *Playboy*, March 1990

"Well, if I ever ran for office, I'd do better as a Democrat than as a Republican—and that's not because I'd be more liberal, because I'm conservative. But the working guy would elect me. He likes me. When I walk down the street, those cabbies start yelling out their windows."

> *Playboy*, March 1990

On What He Can Promise America

"I won't go there, I promise. I pledge on your show. . . . I will not rename the White House."

Larry King Live, 10/08/99

———

"I will be the greatest jobs president that God has ever created."

Campaign launch rally, 6/16/15

On His Political Experience

"Hard to believe I've been a politician for three months, right?"

South Carolina rally, 10/19/15

On the Presidential Polls

"I'm leading big in every poll and we are going to WIN! Remember, Trump NEVER gives up!"

Twitter, @realDonaldTrump, 5:17 p.m., 10/10/15

"I love polls. And somebody said, 'He talks about polls, and the other people don't.' That's because I'm winning! The other people are losing."

Campaign event in Las Vegas, 10/08/15

"A big POLL will be announced this morning on @CBSNews Face The Nation. I wonder if I do well if the press will report the results? Doubt it"

Twitter, @realDonaldTrump, 2:48 p.m., 10/25/15

On His Vice Presidential Pick

"Oprah, I love Oprah. Oprah would always be my first choice."

Larry King Live, 10/08/99

On Political Correctness

"I think the big problem this country has is being politically correct. I've been challenged by so many people and I don't, frankly, have time for total political correctness."

Fox News Republican debate, 08/06/15

"It's very time-consuming to be politically correct. And I don't have the time. It's also very boring to be politically correct. Right? You wouldn't be here if I was totally politically correct."

Hollywood Reporter, 8/19/15

On Why He Wouldn't Win

"And, you know, there's a real good chance, no matter what happens, I won't win. Because, you know, one of these blood-sucking politicians who's been bullshitting people for years will end up—you know, getting elected."

Campaign event in Las Vegas, 4/28/11

On Running for President

"Nobody thought I was gonna run. They said, 'Why would he run? He's got a great life, he's got a beautiful family, he's got a great company.'"

South Carolina rally, 10/19/15

"Don't forget. When I filed, everyone said, 'Well, maybe he won't file, maybe he's not as big as we thought.' Turns out, I'm much bigger. When I filed they, they couldn't believe the numbers. In fact, I was going to file even if I didn't run, I'll be honest with you."

South Carolina rally, 10/19/15

———

"I love my business. I didn't want to do this. I just see our country as going to hell. And I felt I had to do it."

60 Minutes, 9/27/15

On Why People Would Vote for Him

"To be blunt, people would vote for me. 'They just would.' Why? Maybe because I'm so good looking."

New York Times, 9/19/99

On Successful Campaigning

"And did you notice that baby was crying through half of the speech and I didn't get angry? Not once. Did you notice that? That baby was driving me crazy. I didn't get angry once

because I didn't want to insult the parents for not taking the kid out of the room!"

Iowa rally, 4/28/15

On Fixing America

"Look at evangelicals, you can't even use the word 'Christmas' any more, Macy's doesn't use the word 'Christmas.' I mean, you can't even use the word 'Christmas' anymore. And you know, with me, it is going to stop, it is going to stop, and they understand that."

The Economist, 9/03/15

On Making America Great Again

"We're going to have so many victories, you will be bored of winning."

New York Times Magazine, 10/04/15

—

"We're going to have a dynamic country. We're going to have dynamic economics. And it's going to be something really special. And people are going back to work."

Fox News Sunday, 10/18/15

"The line of 'Make America great again,' the phrase, that was mine, I came up with it about a year ago, and I kept using it, and everybody's using it, they are all loving it. I don't know I guess I should copyright it, maybe I have copyrighted it."[*]

MyFox New York, March 2015

"I've actually trademarked it . . . I mean, I get tremendous raves for that line. . . . I could come up with different lines. You would think they would come up with their own. That is my whole theme."

Daily Mail Online, May 2015

---

* "Let's Make America Great Again" was one of Ronald Reagan's most well-known campaign slogans.

On His Opponents

"The thing I'm most honored about is every single person that went after me, including Jeb Bush, who's down. Boom. Every single person that went after me has gone way down. And I'm very honored by that."

Fox News Sunday, 10/18/15

On Hillary Clinton

"If Hillary Clinton can't satisfy her husband what makes her think she can satisfy America?"

>Twitter, @realDonaldTrump, 5:22 p.m., 4/16/15

"She stays in Trump Tower when she's in New York. Not because of me, but because of somebody else who has an apartment in Trump Tower. At least she has good taste."

>*Late Edition with Wolf Blitzer*, 11/28/99

"Hillary Clinton was the worst secretary of state in the history of the United States."

>Interview with Katy Tur, NBC News, 7/08/15

"The concept of . . . [Hilary Clinton's] listening tour is ridiculous. People want ideas. Do you think Winston Churchill, when he was stopping Hitler, went around listening?"

>*New York Times*, 9/19/99

On Jeb Bush

"He's very, very weak on immigration. Don't forget, remember his statement: 'They come for love.' I said, what? Come for love? You got these people coming—half of 'em are criminals. They're coming for love? They're coming for a lot of other reasons, and it's not love."

Iowa Freedom Summit, 1/24/15

———

"Jeb said, 'we were safe with my brother. We were safe.' Well, the World Trade Center just fell down! Now, am I trying to blame him? I'm not blaming anybody. But the World Trade Center came down. So when he said, we were safe, that's not safe."

Fox News Sunday, 10/18/15

———

"Jeb Bush, he has no clue [about immigration issues]. He's never going to be able to do anything."

This Week with George Stephanopoulos, 8/23/15

———

"Jeb Bush just said about Marco Rubio, "he's my friend!" Pure political speak. Why can't he be truthful and say "disloyal guy, no friend!""

Twitter, @realDonaldTrump, 12:30 p.m., 11/05/15

"Jeb's new slogan – "Jeb can fix it". I never thought of Jeb as a crook! Stupid message, the word "fix" is not a good one to use in politics!"

> Twitter, @realDonaldTrump, 8:48 a.m., 11/01/15

"#JebBush has to like Mexican illegals because of his wife."

> Twitter, @realDonaldTrump, 7:39 p.m., 4/04/15

On Carly Fiorina

"Look at that face! Would anyone vote for that? Can you imagine that, the face of our next president?"

> *Rolling Stone*, 9/09/15

"I think she's got a beautiful face and I think she's a beautiful woman."

> CNN Republican debate, 9/16/15

"I just realized that if you listen to Carly Fiorina for more than ten minutes straight, you develop a massive headache. She has zero chance!"

> Twitter, @realDonaldTrump, 12:06 p.m., 8/09/15

On Marco Rubio

"He's weak on immigration—unbelievably weak on immigration, and I'm all about strong on illegal immigration, and other things."

O'Reilly Factor, 9/29/15

On Rand Paul

"First of all, Rand Paul shouldn't even be on this stage. He's number eleven, he's got 1 percent in the polls, and how he got up here—there's far too many people anyway."

CNN Republican debate, 9/16/15

———

"I never attacked him on his looks, and believe me, there's plenty of subject matter right there."

CNN Republican debate, 9/16/15

———

"Truly weird Senator Rand Paul of Kentucky reminds me of a spoiled brat without a properly functioning brain. He was terrible at DEBATE!"

Twitter, @realDonaldTrump, 5:41 p.m., 8/10/15

On Ben Carson

"I don't know Ben Carson. He was a doctor. Perhaps a—you know, an okay doctor, by the way, you can check that out, too. We—they're not talking about a grea [*sic*]—he was an okay doctor."

New Day, CNN, 9/09/15

On Lindsey Graham

"You have a lot of people that are not doing well in that poll, I have to tell—you have a lot of zeros. You know, zero, zero, zero. Do you know who we have that has a zero? Lindsey Graham. What's going on with this guy?"

South Carolina rally, 10/19/15

——

"Congrats @LindseyGrahmSC. You just got 4 points in your home state of SC—far better than zero nationally. You're only 26 pts behind me."

Twitter, @realDonaldTrump, 6:19 p.m., 8/25/15

On John Kasich

"He was so nice. He was such a nice guy. And he said, 'Oh, I'm never gonna attack.' But then his poll numbers tanked, he's got very—that's why he's on the end—and he got nasty. And he got nasty. So you know what? You can have him."

CNBC Republican debate, 10/28/15

On Rick Santorum

"I have a big plane. . . . He doesn't."

Des Moines Register, 4/08/15

On Rick Perry

"He's doing very poorly in the polls. He put on glasses so people will think he's smart. And it just doesn't work! You know, people can see through the glasses."

South Carolina rally, 7/21/15

On His Opponents' Policies on Immigration

"Remember that Carson, Bush and Rubio are VERY weak on illegal immigration. They will do NOTHING to stop it. Our country will be overrun!"

Twitter, @realDonaldTrump, 12:19 a.m., 10/26/15

On Why He's a Unique Candidate

"I'm the most successful person ever to run for the presidency, by far. Nobody's ever been more successful than me. I'm the most successful person ever to run. Ross Perot isn't successful like me. Romney—I have a Gucci store that's worth more than Romney."

Des Moines Register, 6/02/15

On Other Politicians

"Barney Frank looked disgusting--nipples protruding--in his blue shirt before Congress. Very very disrespectful."

Twitter, @realDonaldTrump, 12:36 p.m., 12/21/11

On Al Gore

"I always said he was very, very underrated."

Late Edition with Wolf Blitzer, 11/28/99

On Bill Clinton

"People would have been more forgiving if he'd had an affair with a really beautiful woman of sophistication. Kennedy and Marilyn Monroe were on a different level. Now Clinton can't get into golf clubs in Westchester. A former President begging to get in a golf club. It's unthinkable"

New York Times, 9/19/99

On John Kerry

"He's in a bicycle race, he's seventy-three years old. Seventy-three years old! And I said it the last time I spoke. I swear to you, I will never enter a bicycle race if I'm president. I swear.

I swear! He—he's in a bicycle race. He falls and breaks his leg. This is our chief negotiator. He's walking in and they're looking at him thinking what a schmuck."

Iowa rally, 8/25/15

On Mario Cuomo

"My screaming was so loud that two or three people came in from adjoining offices and asked who I was screaming at. I told them it was Mario Cuomo, a total stiff, a lousy governor, and a disloyal former friend. Now whenever I see Mario at a dinner, I refuse to acknowledge him, talk to him, or even look at him."

Trump: How To Get Rich, 2004

On John McCain

"[John McCain is] . . . not a war hero. He's a war hero—he's a war hero 'cause he was captured. I like people that weren't captured, OK, I hate to tell you."

Iowa Family Leadership Summit, 7/18/15

On Condoleezza Rice

"I see Condoleezza Rice—she goes on a plane, she gets off a plane, she waves, she goes there to meet some dictator. . . . They talk, she leaves, she waves, the plane takes off. Nothing happens, it's a joke, nothing ever happens. I think she's a very nice woman, but I don't want a nice woman. I want someone that's not necessarily nice."

Hannity's America, January 2007

On Mitt Romney

"Why would anybody listen to @MittRomney? He lost an election that should have easily been won against Obama. By the way, so did John McCain!"

Twitter, @realDonaldTrump, 1:16 a.m., 7/19/15

On Sarah Palin

"I'd love [to have her in my cabinet] . . . because she really is somebody who knows what's happening and she's a special person. She's really a special person and I think people know that."

The Palin Update, Mama Grizzly Radio, 7/27/15

On Ronald Reagan

"He is so smooth and so effective a performer that he completely won over the American people. Only now, nearly seven years later, are people beginning to question whether there's anything beneath that smile."

Trump: The Art of the Deal, 1987

On Donald Rumsfeld

"I mean, obviously, Rumsfeld was a disaster."

The Situation Room with Wolf Blitzer, 3/16/07

On Political Tactics

"I know politicians who love women who don't even want to be known for that, because they might lose the gay vote, OK?"

Playboy, March 1990

On the Media

"You know, some of the media is among the worst people I've ever met. I mean a pretty good percentage is really a terrible group of people."

60 Minutes, 9/27/15

On Megyn Kelly

"You could see there was blood coming out of her eyes, blood coming out of her wherever."

CNN Tonight, 6/07/15

———

"[With my comment,] I was referring to—or, if I finished it, I was going to say, 'ears,' or 'nose,' because that's a common statement."

Today, 8/10/15

On Arianna Huffington

".@ariannahuff is unattractive both inside and out. I fully understand why her former husband left her for a man- he made a good decision."

Twitter, @realDonaldTrump, 10:54 a.m., 8/28/12

On Reporters

"Uncomfortable looking NBC reporter Willie Geist calls me to ask for favors and then mockingly smiles when he is told of my high poll numbers."

> Twitter, @realDonaldTrump, 5:36 p.m., 6/24/15

———

"One of the dumbest political pundits on television is Chris Stirewalt of @FoxNews. Wrong facts - check Fox debate rankings, Trump #1. Dope!"

> Twitter, @realDonaldTrump, 8:50 a.m., 11/07/15

———

"You have, I'd say, 10 to 15 to 20 percent who are truly bad people. They're dishonest, they're horrible human beings. They know—it's not a question of being lazy or anything— they actually go out of their way to write false stories."

> Virginia rally, 10/14/15

On Getting Media

"The point is that if you are a little different, or a little outrageous, or if you do things that are bold or controversial, the press is going to write about you."

Trump: The Art Of The Deal, 1987

———

"I've really been focused much more on the news shows lately, on Fox and CNN and even MSNBC, which is doing better because they're covering me all the time."

Hollywood Reporter, 9/03/15

———

"You know, look, I'm on a lot of covers. I think maybe more than almost any supermodel. I think more than any supermodel. But in a way that is a sign of respect, people are respecting what you are doing."

60 Minutes, 9/27/15

On Handling Reporters

"I'd love to grab some of these guys, I really would. I really want them to make a mistake, because I really would like to do it. Not because I'm a suer, but I would really love to be able to knock a couple of them out."

Larry King Live, 1990

On Criticism

"I'm a counterpuncher. I don't have a choice. If you look what they say about me, it's terrible. I mean, they say terrible things about me."

Fox News Sunday, 10/18/15

On Pop Culture

"My favorite part [of *Pulp Fiction*] is when Sam has his gun out in the diner and he tells the guy to tell his girlfriend to shut up. Tell that bitch to be cool. Say: 'Bitch be cool.' I love those lines."

Donald Trump, as quoted in *TrumpNation: The Art Of Being The Donald*, 2005

On Celebrity Romance

"Robert Pattinson should not take back Kristen Stewart. She cheated on him like a dog & will do it again--just watch. He can do much better!"

> Twitter, @realDonaldTrump, 2:47 p.m., 10/17/12

"Everyone knows I am right that Robert Pattinson should dump Kristen Stewart. In a couple of years, he will thank me. Be smart, Robert."

> Twitter, @realDonaldTrump, 12:18 a.m., 10/23/12

".@katyperry Katy, what the hell were you thinking when you married loser Russell Brand. There is a guy who has got nothing going, a waste!"

> Twitter, @realDonaldTrump, 7:52 p.m., 10/17/14

On Women in Hollywood

"Cher is somewhat of a loser. She's lonely. She's unhappy. She's very miserable."

On the Record with Greta Van Susteren, 5/14/12

———

"While @BetteMidler is an extremely unattractive woman, I refuse to say that because I always insist on being politically correct."

Twitter, @realDonaldTrump, 7:29 p.m., 10/28/12

On Rosie O'Donnell

"Rosie's a person who's very lucky to have her girlfriend. And she better be careful, or I'll send one of my friends over to pick up her girlfriend. Why would she stay with Rosie if she had another choice?"

Entertainment Tonight, 12/21/06

———

"Well, Rosie O'Donnell's disgusting, both inside and out. You take a look at her, she's a slob. She talks like a truck driver."

Entertainment Tonight, 12/21/06

"I loved it. I gloat over it. I think it's wonderful, because I like to see bad people fail. Rosie failed? I'm happy about it."

Entertainment Tonight, 12/21/06

"Probably I'll sue her, because it would be fun. I'd like to take some money out of her fat-ass pockets."

Entertainment Tonight, 12/21/06

"If I were running *The View*, I'd fire Rosie. I mean, I'd look at her right in that fat, ugly face of hers and say, 'Rosie, you're fired.' We're all a little chubby, but Rosie's just worse than most of us."

Entertainment Tonight, 12/21/06

On Jon Stewart

"I promise you that I'm much smarter than Jonathan Lei-bowitz - I mean Jon Stewart @TheDailyShow. Who, by the way, is totally overrated."

Twitter, @realDonaldTrump, 8:09 p.m., 4/24/13

"All the haters and losers must admit that, unlike others, I never attacked dopey Jon Stewart for his phony last name. Would never do that!"

> Twitter, @realDonaldTrump, 7:33 p.m. 5/30/15

———

"While Jon Stewart is a joke, not very bright and totally overrated, some losers and haters will miss him & his dumb clown humor. Too bad!"

> Twitter, @realDonaldTrump, 8:49 p.m., 6/01/15

On Being on TV

"Jay Leno and his people are constantly calling me to go on his show. My answer is always no because his show sucks. They love my ratings!"

> Twitter, @realDonaldTrump, 8:46 a.m., 9/05/13

———

"What is it about me that gets Larry King his highest ratings?"

> *TrumpNation: The Art of Being The Donald*, 2005

On Larry King's Breath

"Do you mind if I sit back a little bit? Because your breath is very bad. It really is. Has this ever been told to you before?"

Larry King Live, 4/15/89

On Kim Kardashian

"In the old days, they'd say she's got a bad body."

The Howard Stern Show, 6/17/14

On Bill Cosby

"I was never a fan. His humor was always, like, slow and stupid to me . . . I think he's weird. And I never found his humor good at all. Just sit in a chair, talk very slowly? And I say to myself, 'What's this all about?'"

Hollywood Reporter, 8/19/15

On Television Shows

"The Oscars are a sad joke, very much like our President. So many things are wrong!"

> Twitter, @realDonaldTrump, 8:56 a.m., 2/23/15

———

"Just tried watching Modern Family - written by a moron, really boring. Writer has the mind of a very dumb and backward child. Sorry Danny!"

> Twitter, @realDonaldTrump, 6:16 a.m., 6/13/13

On Business

"For me, business comes easier than relationships."

Esquire, January 2004

On Making Deals

"Deals are people."

O'Reilly Factor, 9/28/14

———

"The worst thing you can possibly do in a deal is seem desperate to make it. That makes the other guy smell blood, and then you're dead."

Trump: The Art of The Deal, 1987

———

"The art of the deal. There's nothing like it."

South Carolina rally, 10/19/15

On Business Relationships

"I play to people's fantasies. People may not always think big themselves, but they can still get very excited by those who do. That's why a little hyperbole never hurts. People want to

believe that something is the biggest and the greatest and the most spectacular."

The Art of the Deal, 1987

On Making Money

"I say, not in a braggadocios way, I've made billions and billions of dollars dealing with people all around the world."

CNN Republican debate, 9/16/15

———

"I was a businessman all my life. I've made a tremendous fortune."

This Week with George Stephanopoulos, 8/02/15

———

"Money was never a big motivation for me, except as a way to keep score. The real excitement is playing the game!"

Twitter, @realDonaldTrump 7:38 p.m., 9/14/14

On Working with the Miss Universe Pageant

"The [1997] pageant [was] in Miami Beach, my first as owner, was a huge success. We'd sold out the house; it was a mob

76

scene. From my position offstage, I was able to glance up to the greenroom occasionally. I could just see Alicia Machado, the current Miss Universe, sitting there plumply. God, what problems I had with this woman. First, she wins. Second, she gains fifty pounds. Third, I urge the committee not to fire her. Fourth, I go to the gym with her, in a show of support. Final act: She trashes me in *The Washington Post*—after I stood by her the entire time. What's wrong with this picture? Anyway, the best part about the evening was the knowledge that next year, she would no longer be Miss Universe."

Trump: The Art of the Comeback, 1997

On Not Winning

"I do whine because I want to win, and I'm not happy about not winning, and I am a whiner, and I keep whining and whining until I win."

New Day, CNN, 8/10/15

On Sharing His Financial Success

"I look very much forward to showing my financials, because they are huge."

TIME, 4/14/11

"If you don't tell people about your success, they probably won't know about it."

Trump: How to Get Rich, 2004

On Shaking Hands

"I think the handshake is barbaric . . . Shaking hands, you catch the flu, you catch this, you catch all sorts of things."

TIME, 11/08/99

"The concept of shaking hands is absolutely terrible, and statistically I've been proven right."

Playboy, October 2004

"Something very important, and indeed society changing, may come out of the Ebola epidemic that will be a very good thing: NO SHAKING HANDS!"

Twitter, @realDonaldTrump, 10:14 a.m., 10/04/14

"Know what? After shaking five thousand hands, I think I'll go wash mine."

New Yorker, 5/19/97

On Himself

"I can't help it that I'm a celebrity. What am I going to do, hide under a stone?"

USA Today, 2/27/04

On His Intelligence

"I am a really smart guy."

TIME, 4/14/11

"I'm intelligent. Some people would say I'm very, very, very intelligent."

Fortune, 4/03/00

"Sorry losers and haters, but my I.Q. is one of the highest -and you all know it! Please don't feel so stupid or insecure,it's not your fault"

Twitter, @realDonaldTrump, 9:37 p.m., 5/09/13

"I know some of you may think I'm tough and harsh but actually I'm a very compassionate person (with a very high IQ) with strong common sense"

Twitter, @realDonaldTrump, 10:05 a.m., 4/21/13

"I'm a very smart guy. Went to the best college, I had good marks. I was a very smart guy, good student, all that stuff."

O'Reilly Factor, 2011

On His Appeal

"It's very possible that I could be the first presidential candidate to run and make money on it."

Fortune, 4/03/00

———

"I know what sells and I know what people want."

Playboy, March 1990

On Figuring Him Out

"Who knows what's in the deepest part of my mind?"

BuzzFeed, 2/13/14

On Self-Maintenance

"I think Viagra is wonderful if you need it, if you have medical issues, if you've had surgery. I've just never needed it. Frankly, I wouldn't mind if there were an anti-Viagra, something with the opposite effect. I'm not bragging. I'm just lucky. I don't need it."

Playboy, October 2004

"I scrape the toppings off my pizza—I never eat the dough."

Us Weekly, 9/17/15

On His Hair

"I get up, take a shower, and wash my hair. Then I read the newspapers and watch the news on television, and slowly the hair dries. It takes about an hour. I don't use a blow-dryer. Once it's dry I comb it. Once I have it the way I like it—even though nobody else likes it—I spray it and it's good for the day."

Playboy, October 2004

"No animals have been harmed in the creation of my hair-style."

Trump: How to Get Rich, 2004

———

"As everybody knows, but the haters & losers refuse to acknowledge, I do not wear a "wig." My hair may not be perfect but it's mine."

Twitter, @realDonaldTrump, 7:40 p.m., 4/24/14

On What Makes Him Great

"Part of the beauty of me is that I am very rich."

Good Morning America, 3/17/11

———

"Some people have a talent for piano. Some people have a talent for raising a family. Some people have a talent for golf. I just happen to have a talent for making money."

Playboy, October 2004

———

"I don't think I'm ambitious. I think I'm—I'm somebody that enjoys so much what he's doing."

60 Minutes, 1985

"A lot of people see psychiatrists because they don't have enough on their mind. I spend so much time thinking about buildings and deals and clubs and doing what I do that I don't have time to get into trouble mentally."

Playboy, October 2004

"I never fall for scams. I am the only person who immediately walked out of my 'Ali G' interview"

Twitter, @realDonaldTrump, 9:14 p.m., 9/30/12

On His People Skills

"I'm actually a nice person. I try very hard to be a nice person."

Fox News, 9/28/14

On His Influence

"My twitter has become so powerful that I can actually make my enemies tell the truth."

Twitter, @realDonaldTrump, 6:36 p.m., 9/17/12

On Who Should Play Him in a Movie

"Somebody really, really handsome. That's the only thing that matters. I don't care if he can act well. He's got to be really, really good-looking. OK?"

Hollywood Reporter, 9/03/15

On His Free Time

"I enjoy testing friendships."

Playboy, March 1990

———

"I don't have a lot of time for listening to television."

New York Times, 6/28/15

———

"If I'm on a show, I'll turn on the show."

60 Minutes, 9/27/15

———

"I love just being home, relaxing, taking it easy, watching television. And maybe, necessarily, if there's pizza, that's good, too."

Early Noon, 7/26/89

"I've never gambled in my life. To me, a gambler is someone who plays slot machines. I prefer to own slot machines."

Trump: The Art of the Deal, 1987

On Getting to Know Him

"I don't think of myself as driven."

Late Night With David Letterman, 1987

"My life essentially is one big, fat phone call."

Esquire, January 2004

"I photograph short. I'm 6 foot 3."

New York Times, 9/19/99

"People say the '80s are dead, all the luxury, the extravagance. I say, 'What?' am I supposed to change my taste because it's a new decade? That's bullshit."

Playboy, March 1997

"I think I'm a very honest guy, and in fact, maybe too honest to be a politician."

Late Edition with Wolf Blitzer, 11/28/99

———

"I'm only thin-skinned when somebody says bad things that are false."

Fox News Sunday, 10/18/15

———

"I don't like doing a lot of talking. I like—believe it or not—I like action."

The Herd with Colin Cowherd, 11/02/15

On Romance

"Oftentimes when I was sleeping with one of the top women in the world, I would say to myself, thinking about me as a boy from Queens, 'Can you believe what I am getting?'"

Think Big: Make It Happen In Business and Life, 2008

———

"All of the women on the *Apprentice* flirted with me—consciously or unconsciously. That's to be expected."

Trump: How To Get Rich, 2004

"If I told the real stories of my experiences with women, often seemingly very happily married and important women, this book would be a guaranteed best-seller (which it will be anyway!). I'd love to tell all, using names and places, but I just don't think it's right."

Trump: The Art of the Comeback, 1994

"I've never had any trouble in bed, but if I'd had affairs with half the starlets and female athletes the newspapers linked me with, I'd have no time to breathe."

Trump: Surviving at the Top, 1990

"Certain guys tell me they want women of substance, not beautiful models. It just means they can't get beautiful models."

New York Times, 9/19/99

On Break-ups

"When a man leaves a woman, especially when it was perceived that he has left for a piece of ass—a good one!—there

are 50 percent of the population who will love the woman who was left."

Vanity Fair, September 1990

On the People Who Like Him

"The fact is, I go down the streets of New York and the people that really like me are the taxi drivers and the workers, etc, etc."

Interview with Larry King at the Republican National
Convention, 1988

———

"There are two publics as far as I'm concerned. The real public and then there's the New York society horseshit. The real public has always liked Donald Trump."

Vanity Fair, September 1990

———

"The rich people hate me and the workers love me. Now, the rich people that know me like me, but the rich people that don't know me, they truly dislike me."

Larry King Live, 10/08/99

———

"Wealthy people don't like me, 'cause I'm competing against them all the time, and they don't like me, and I like to win."
Interview with Larry King at the Republican National Convention, 1988

On Family

"She does have a very nice figure. . . . If [Ivanka] weren't my daughter, perhaps I'd be dating her."

The View, 2006

———

"You know who's one of the great beauties of the world, according to everybody? And I helped create her. Ivanka. My daughter, Ivanka. She's six feet tall, she's got the best body. She made a lot money as a model—a tremendous amount."

The Howard Stern Show, 2003

———

"Every guy in the country wants to go out with my daughter."

New York Magazine, 12/13/04

On Marriage

"Of course, if necessary, I could be married in twenty-four hours. . . . It would be very easy. Believe me."

New York Times, 9/19/99

———

"My marriage, it seemed, was the only area of my life in which I was willing to accept something less than perfection."

Trump: Surviving at the Top, 1990

———

"I would never buy Ivana any decent jewels or pictures. Why give her negotiable assets?"

Vanity Fair, September 1990

On Parents

"I was always very much accepted by my father. He adored Donald Trump."

Playboy, March 1990

On Children

"I want five children, like in my own family, because with five, then I will know that one will be guaranteed to turn out like me."

Vanity Fair, September 1990

On Life Lessons

"Let golf be elitist. When I say 'aspire,' that's a positive word. Let people work hard and aspire to someday be able to play golf."

Fortune, 7/01/15

On Life Lessons

"People say, 'Well, money can't buy happiness.' And they're absolutely right. But it does make it easier."

Early Noon, 7/26/89

———

"You can't con people, at least not for long. You can create excitement, you can do wonderful promotion and get all kinds of press, and you can throw in a little hyperbole. But if you don't deliver the goods, people will eventually catch on."

Trump: The Art of the Deal, 1987

———

"You need energy. In life, you need energy as well as brains. Brains is always number one, but you need energy."

Larry King Live, 1990

———

"I truly believe that someone successful is never really happy, because dissatisfaction is what drives him."

Playboy, March 1990

———

"I like the challenge and tell the story of the coal miner's son. The coal miner gets black-lung disease, his son gets it, then his son. If I had been the son of a coal miner, I would have left the damn mines."

Playboy, March 1990

—

"I have never seen a thin person drinking Diet Coke."

Twitter, @realDonaldTrump, 10:13 p.m., 10/14/12

On Gender Relationship

"Women are much tougher and more calculating than men. I relate better to women."

New York Times, 9/19/99

On Being Right

"I think I'm right. And when I think I'm right, nothing bothers me."

60 Minutes, 1985

On Loyalty

"I really believe in trashing your enemies and really being loyal to your friends. I'm a strong believer in loyalty."

Early Noon, 7/26/89

On Tough Times

"Hey, look, I had a cold spell from 1990 to '91. I was beat up in business and in my personal life. But you learn that you're either the toughest, meanest piece of shit in the world or you just crawl into a corner, put your finger in your mouth, and say, 'I want to go home.' You never know until you're under pressure how you're gonna react. Guys that I thought were tough were *nothing*.'"

New York Magazine, 8/15/94

On Egos

"Show me someone with no ego and I'll show you a big loser."

Trump: How To Get Rich, 2004

"I have an ego, but all people that are successful have an ego. I've never met a successful person that didn't have an ego."

Larry King Live, 1990

On Jealousy

"One of the problems when you become successful is that jealousy and envy inevitably follow. There are people—I categorize them as life's losers—who get their sense of accomplishment and achievement from trying to stop others. As far as I'm concerned, if they had any real ability they wouldn't be fighting me, they'd be doing something constructive themselves."

Trump: The Art of the Deal, 1987

On Borrowing

"As a kid, I was making a building with blocks in our playroom. I didn't have enough. So I asked my younger brother, Robert, if I could borrow some of his. He said, 'Okay, but you have to give them back when you're done.' I used all of my blocks, then all of his blocks, and when I was done I had

a great building, which I then glued together. Robert never did get those blocks back."

Esquire, January 2004

On Winning

"If you don't win you can't get away with it. And I win, I win, I always win. In the end, I always win, whether it's in golf, whether it's in tennis, whether it's in life, I just always win. And I tell people I always win, because I do."

TrumpNation: The Art of Being The Donald, 2005

About the Authors

Seth Millstein is a political journalist whose work has been published by media such as *Bustle*, *The Daily*, and *Huffington Post*. He lives in Oakland, CA.

Bill Katovsky was a journalist and editor, and the author of books such as *The World According to Gore*, *Patriots Act*, and *Embedded: The Media at War in Iraq*. He worked in media for more than thirty-one years, and passed away in November 2015.

Trumpisms is dedicated to Bill Katovsky and all others willing to make candid assessments of our politicians.

Special thanks are due to Lois Katovsky and Timothy Carlson.